James
Butler
Bonham

James Butler Bonham

The Rebel Hero

Jean Flynn

Illustrations by G. E. Buddy Mullan

EAKIN PRESS
Austin, Texas

FIRST EDITION

Copyright © 1984
By Jean Flynn

Published in the United States of America
By Eakin Press, P.O. Box 23066, Austin, Texas 78735

ISBN 0-89015-511-9

For Gladys Flynn

CONTENTS

CHAPTER 1

The Mischief-Maker

"Stop squirming around, Milledge, or I'm gonna drop you in the mud," Jim warned his small brother. Jim was carrying Milledge piggyback to school.

"But my feet are cold," Milledge complained.

Jim shifted the small boy higher on his back and stuck his brother's cold, bare feet into his pockets. "Now don't say your stinky feet are crooked and hurt or I'll sure enough drop you in the mud. I told you to wear shoes."

"My feet don't stink," Milledge argued.

"Well, they will after you walk in the mud a mile," Jim laughed. He pretended to stumble and let Milledge slip as if he were falling.

"Don't drop me! Don't drop me!" Milledge screamed. He clung to Jim like an opossum to a tree.

"Auggg! You're choking me. I can't breathe!" Jim croaked and stumbled along the path. Milledge knew then that Jim was teasing him again. What the young boy did not know was that the game his older brother played with him was to take Milledge's mind off of how cold and miserable he was.

James Butler Bonham didn't think of his own discomfort as he carried his barefoot brother to school. He was too busy planning how he could make his own day exciting.

Jim came from ancestors who lived in a time of rebellion and excitement. The Bonham family can be traced back to Nicholas Bonham who married Hannah Fuller on January 1659, at Barnstable, Massachusetts. Hannah's father, Samuel Fuller, was one of the children on the *Mayflower*. The Bonham children from that marriage moved to Kentucky and South Carolina.

Jim's father, James Bonham, moved to South Carolina after the American Revolution. He was the great-great-grandson of Nicholas. James Bonham served in the Revolutionary War. He fought the British the same way and for the same reason that his son would fight the Mexicans for Texas Independence.

The older James Bonham was a soldier with the rank of private in a Maryland Cavalry Company at the age of fifteen. He served at the Siege of Yorktown. His captain was only nineteen years old. He spent several years in the tidewater region of South Carolina and finally settled in the valley of the Saluda River where he became a wealthy and respected planter.

James Bonham chose his new homestead with care. The Saluda River was in the Piedmont Plateau. The region was an area of gently rolling to hilly land lying between the Appalachian Mountains and the Atlantic Coastal Plains. It was a rich, fertile area for growing cotton.

The textile industry was just beginning to become a major industry. In 1790, Samuel Slater, a textile worker and mechanic from England, built a machine that converted raw cotton into threads and cloth. Eli Whitney invented the cotton gin in 1793. The cotton gin made it possible to send more raw cotton to the textile mills.

As the demand for cotton increased, James Bonham bought more slaves to gather the crops. He built a beautiful plantation home. The two-story plantation house was put together with wooden pegs. There were no nails used in the entire structure. The handcarved mantle pieces were the talk of the community.

Bonham's first wife was Hanna Wetzel. They had a son, John, and a daughter, Annie. Hanna died very young, leaving the young man with the two children.

Bonham, a handsome landowner, then married Sophia Smith. They had eight children, five sons and three daughters. James Butler Bonham, hero of the Alamo, was the fourth son born to Sophia and James.

James Butler Bonham was born February 20, 1807, at Red Bank, Edgefield County, South Carolina.

When Jim was eight years old his father died. His stepbrother and stepsister were already grown and away from home. His mother inherited a comfortable estate from her father as well as her husband. She was a good manager and very competently ran both estates. Jim grew up in a large plantation home not lacking for comfort.

There were no schools except for "field schools" which the Bonham children attended. The field schools were centrally located in an area of plantations. The one room building was constructed of logs or wood frame. A huge potbelly stove stood in the middle of the room. Each cold day some of the larger boys carried wood inside from the huge pile that was cut and stacked on the outside of the schoolroom.

Chairs, benches and desks were crudely made by landowners' carpenters and slaves. If the teacher were a woman, she couldn't be married. She lived with one of the families as part of her wages. The teacher knew all of the parents of her students. Jim Bonham knew he couldn't get away with a thing if she knew for sure who did something.

Jim was not a bad boy but he was rebellious. He had no problems learning but he couldn't see the need to waste time in the schoolroom. His mother was as spirited as he was so he went to school. He had great respect and admiration for his mother.

Jim decided school was not all that bad. His best friend was William Barret Travis — sometimes called "Buck" by his family and friends. Buck lived on another plantation about five miles from Jim. Although Buck was two years younger than Jim, they became fast friends. What mischief one couldn't think of, the other one did. Both of the boys were adventurous and impetuous. They did not always think through what they were doing. They often acted quickly. They often found themselves in trouble.

They were both intelligent young men. They learned faster than anyone in the school when they set their minds to do it. They could think up more mischief than anyone else. The teacher liked both of the young boys. Their pranks were harmless, but even she reached a point when Jim and Buck knew they had gone too far.

"Eeeek!" screamed a young girl as she wildly waved her arms. A huge toad jumped to the floor. The toad's black eyes bulged. Low croaking sounds filled the schoolroom when the screaming girl ran out of breath. Startled children looked from the pale, frightened girl to the frightened, croaking toad. It was hard to tell which was the most scared — the girl or the toad.

Everyone was surprised except Jim and Buck. They could not hide smiles.

4

"Jim, since you brought the toad inside, you may take it outside," the teacher's voice was firm.

Jim Bonham did not deny that he had carried the toad into the room and placed it inside the girl's desk. He walked slowly behind the toad. He stopped within an arm's length of it. Quicker than the eye could follow, he caught the toad by the back. No one dared to laugh, but the teacher knew they would learn nothing until they had had a chance to talk and laugh about Jim and Buck's latest escapade. No one doubted that they were behind the prank. The teacher waited silently until Jim returned empty-handed.

"Today we will have an early dinner," she told the class. "There will be no noise until you are outside. Class dismissed, *except* for Jim and Buck." No question about it, they were in trouble again.

The children grabbed their home-packed dinners and hurried out the door. Their laughter sounded loud in the quiet schoolroom. Jim and Buck stood before the teacher. They were beginning to squirm before she spoke. This was the first time she had looked so angry. Before, she had made them stay in during recess and write lines. Sometimes she made them sweep and clean the room or carry water.

They had been carrying water when Jim found the toad near the well. Their punishment for playing hooky the week before was to keep drinking water in the schoolroom for a month. That was no punishment for them, but the teacher did not know that at the time. Now she knew.

"You two are a disgrace to this school!" her low voice trembled with anger. "And you are a disgrace to your families." The boys thought her rage was out of proportion to the misconduct. Jim and Buck knew she couldn't be that angry about the toad. She was angry about *all* of the things they did to stir up excitement. The laughter disappeared from their eyes. They weren't sorry about the toad. They were sorry that the teacher was so upset. They liked and respected her.

When she saw the boys were no longer smiling, she stopped talking. After a minute's silence, she said, "Go eat your dinners," and turned her back to them to look out of the window.

Jim and Buck stood still, uncertain of their punishment. "Is that all?" Jim asked.

"Please leave the room," she answered without turning toward them.

"But, Ma'am," Jim began, only to be interrupted.

"Leave the room," she demanded in a voice edged with fury.

Jim and Buck walked quickly but quietly from the room. The fun of their last joke had turned to disappointment. There was no easy way out for them. No punishment for their prank was the harshest punishment they could have received.

For days they waited anxiously for the teacher to take action. They swore to stick together and face whatever came.

That was not the last time that the two friends took an oath of loyalty to each other. With many years between the country school and the Alamo, they would once again wait anxiously together.

CHAPTER 2

The Rebel Friend

"Why are you leaving?" a breathless Jim demanded as he jumped from a sweaty horse that had stopped abruptly in front of Buck Travis.

"Because my pa has sold our place," a sullen Buck answered. He had watched the dust fly from Jim's horse's hooves as his friend rode up to the house. "We are moving to Alabama Territory. Pa says we can buy more land — better land. He says everybody is moving west."

"Well, we're not!" Jim responded heatedly, "because we have better sense! We don't do things just because some other dunce does it."

When Sophia had told her son that Mark Travis was moving his family, Jim wanted her to move also. Sophia was sensitive to her son's hurt at losing his best friend. She explained that while a man could move to better, more fertile land, a woman alone had more problems.

Sophia had managed her two estates well. She had a

good overseer and plenty of slaves. Her position in the community had been established. She was respected as a businesswoman — which few women were in those days. It would be very difficult for her to become established in an untamed, unsettled, part of the country.

While Sophia was a strong businesswoman, she had a sentimental side that she showed only to her family and close friends.

"You have to understand, son," she had said softly, her eyes misting with tears, "I have more than money invested in this land. Your pa and little Jacob and Elizabeth are buried here." Her eyes turned toward the fenced graveyard in a grove of trees down the road from the house.

Jim had shyly touched his mother's hand. He did not remember his brother Jacob or his sister Elizabeth. They had both died as infants before he was born. He remembered his father's death three years past when he was eight years old. He remembered his mother's sadness and the many times that she carried flowers to put on the graves. He remembered her determination to run the plantations as well as a man.

Now he turned his hurt and anger on his friend Buck. "Why didn't you tell your pa you aren't going? You could live with us if you aren't afraid of wanting your ma."

Nine-year-old Buck Travis lost his sullen look. His ready temper flared, "Well, if you wasn't such a sissy, you'd just pack your saddlebag and come with us. I'm gonna have more fun than puttin' old bug-eyed toads in girls' desks."

"You won't even know how to have fun by yourself," Jim sneered, "because I do all the thinking for you."

"Whoa, you two wild bears," Mark Travis teased and stepped between the two friends who were acting like enemies. "Jim, ask your ma if you can spend Saturday and Sunday with us. You and Buck might get in some good fishing. The fish might even bite on a day that's not a schoolday."

"Yes, sir," Jim looked at the chuckling Mark Travis. He could not keep the gleam of excitement from his eyes. He knew that Mr. Travis was saying they would have a free two days to do just what they wanted to do. Two whole days of camping and fishing with Buck. Well, they would make the most of it.

When the two boys looked into each other's eyes, all quarrels were forgotten. No words were needed to erase their anger. They were already planning their outing together. Jim mounted his horse with a light heart and galloped home.

Sophia eagerly helped her son pack saddlebags for his fishing trip with Buck. She knew the two boys could eat a whole pig when they were hungry. She couldn't count on their catching enough fish to fill their empty stomachs. She wrapped food in a white cloth and tied it at the four corners. When Jim hung the bundle on his saddlehorn, he knew they were in for a treat.

"I wanna go too," cried Milledge who was hanging onto his mother's long cotton skirt. Big tears ran down his unhappy face.

"Why, Milledge, who would help me take care of baby Julie if you left?" Sophia appealed to her five-year-old son. She turned her beautiful face to Jim and nodded her head. "This is your time, son. Be careful."

Jim waved goodbye and slowly rode away from his family. Jim thought about the changes in his life. He was full of confusion and contradictions. He wanted excitement and adventure; yet, he wanted everything to stay the same. He wanted his oldest brother Simeon to become a great lawyer, but he wanted Simeon back home. He wanted his oldest sister Sarah to be happy with her hus-

Young Bonham and Travis go fishing

band but why couldn't they just live on the Bonham plantations? Already Malakiah was talking about moving west and he was just fifteen. Milledge, five, and Julie, three, were still just babies. It would be nice if they could just stay that way awhile. But he knew they could not.

Then Jim thought about himself. He was losing his best friend. Someday he would go west, too. His young, active mind overshadowed his melancholy thoughts.

By the time he met Buck, he had planned a long life of adventure for both of them. He and Buck were going to make their own adventure.

Jim and Buck rode side by side on their spirited horses. They talked about where they were going to set up camp. They knew just the right place on the Saluda River where their horses could graze while they fished.

They tethered and unsaddled their horses. They took their provisions to a campsite under a tall tree where they had built a fire before. Jim had brought a hatchet to chop kindling and wood for their fire. Quickly they set up their camp. Each unrolled his blankets so the warm sun would seep into them for the cool night.

The day went all too quickly. They stopped fishing just long enough to eat a cold dinner. The pemmican cakes Sophia Bonham had packed were a treat. The American settlers had learned how to make the tasty mixture from the Indians. The small cakes were made from dried meat pounded into a powder and mixed with hot fat and dried fruit. Sophia had packed enough for both boys to have their fill. They munched on the cakes and hunks of fried cornbread while they talked about how poor the fishing was.

They were hungry again and about to give up on fishing when Jim caught one more. The sun was slowly sinking when they decided they had fish enough for their supper.

Sparks flew from the flint and the dried kindling and leaves slowly blazed. Jim waited until he was sure the kindling was burning before he stacked a small pyramid of wood to catch the fire.

"Let's clean the fish while the fire burns down," he suggested to Buck.

The boys always carried pocketknives and went to work gutting the fish. Buck took the cleaned fish to the river to wash them while Jim made a spit frame out of green branches to cook them over the fire.

When the fire burned down to glowing coals, Jim raked out a spot and put raw potatoes in the pit he had dug. He covered them with more live coals and placed the speared fish on the spit frame.

The light from the glowing embers of the fire danced on two contented faces. The fish spewed and sputtered as they cooked over the hot coals. The potatoes smelled charred.

Jim and Buck were not just pranksters in school. Both were bright young men and loved reading. As they sat near the fire, turning the fish on the spit, their talk turned to both legendary and real heroes that they admired.

Buck's favorite book hero was Robin Hood, the legendary hero who stole from the rich and gave to the poor. Their talk of Robin Hood and the smell of burned potatoes reminded them of South Carolina's own "Robin Hood," the "Swamp Fox."

"I bet the Swamp Fox was better fighting the Redcoats than Robin Hood," Jim challenged Buck.

"I wish we could have fought with him," Buck answered. He would not argue about which hero had done the most for his people. The Swamp Fox was his hero, too.

General Francis Marion, leader of a guerrilla force in the American Revolution, was called the Swamp Fox because he was as stealthy as a fox. He attacked the British in the dark of the night. His guerrilla force killed, destroyed, and scattered their enemy. Then he and his men disappeared into the depths of the Pee Dee or Santee river swamps. Men who tried to follow them were swallowed in the mirk and mire covered with vines and shadows.

Marion was born on a plantation in Berkeley County, South Carolina, in 1732. He learned fighting strategy in the Cherokee wars. People looked upon him as being the most brilliant guerrilla leader in the American Revolution. And like the age-old Robin Hood of literature, he wanted to help his people.

He was a small, dark and courageous man. He was very independent. Many people loved him and many people hated him. He was loved by his friends and his brigade. He was equally hated and feared by his enemies.

Men looked upon him with great confidence in his leadership ability. Even his enemies respected him as a leader although they feared him. He was always at the head of his forces when he went into battle.

As the young boys cut through the blackened skin of the baked potatoes, they talked about the stories still told of the Swamp Fox, who had died years before they were born. He and his men often ate the same as Jim and Buck were doing. The guerrillas cut slabs of bark to use for plates. They baked their potatoes the same way and felt very fortunate if they had wild game for a meal. They could not waste ammunition on hunting food. Their wives had melted pewter and metal for bullets for the guerrillas. They had none to spare.

The guerrillas had no uniforms. The only thing they had in common was a brown leather cap. Their motto was burned across the front of their caps for all to see:

Victory or Death.

When James Butler Bonham and William Barret Travis spoke so quietly and so reverently of their hero in the still of the night, they did not know that one day the two friends would be bound together with Marion's words, *Victory or Death.*

CHAPTER 3

The Rebel Student

Jim spent a few uneventful years after Buck Travis moved in 1818. He tormented the teacher and occasionally played tricks on his fellow students. He sometimes played hooky when he thought school should have a holiday and the teacher didn't agree.

As the population in South Carolina increased, towns sprang up. Many private schools or academies began to replace the old country or field schools. The Bonham family had the means of transportation to and from school. The children attended academies with good reputations for discipline. Jim needed a strong hand to keep him in line.

The teacher always knew that Jim was going to take the opposite side of every issue. Whatever could be questioned, Jim questioned it. Whatever rule could be tested, Jim tested it. He thrived on rebellion.

Jim and Buck stayed in touch through the years of

young manhood. Jim's half-brother John and his brother Simeon both moved to Alabama and established law practice. Buck Travis had relatives in Edgefield. By one or the other family, the young men stayed in contact and they remained good friends across the miles and time. They were too much alike in temperament for a separation to break their strong bond of friendship.

Around the year 1824, Jim entered South Carolina College which is now the University of South Carolina at Columbia. He was involved more with activities that had nothing to do with his classes than he was with studies.

Jim discovered a living hero in Marquis de Lafayette. Lafayette was a French soldier and statesman. He fought for American independence during the American Revolution, and was an able strategist. He was a prominent leader in revolutionary times in France. He was always a liberal but never became a radical. His actions won the respect of Americans and Frenchmen alike.

Lafayette was born in 1757. His father died in battle when the boy was two years old. When his mother and grandfather died eleven years later, he inherited a great fortune. Lafayette came from a long line of soldiers and studied at the Military Academy in Versailles. At the age of sixteen, he married Adrienne de Noailles, a daughter of one of the most influential families in France. Shortly afterward, Lafayette became a captain in the cavalry.

Lafayette disliked court life. He welcomed the American Revolution as an opportunity to win military glory by fighting against the British. He purchased a ship and landed in America in 1777, with a party of soldier-adventurers. The twenty-year-old marquis impressed the Continental Congress. He was made a major general, without pay, and joined George Washington's staff.

Lafayette was a "hero to two worlds" when he returned to France in 1782. He was influential in both America and in France.

He revisited America in 1784, and stayed at Mount Vernon with Washington. He returned in 1824. Both times a grateful nation received him with enthusiasm.

Jim was in his second year at South Carolina College when Lafayette visited Columbia. A cadet company was formed among the students to parade in his honor. Jim was a member of the corps. Lafayette was Jim's kind of man. A man who was willing to risk everything he had, to fight for what he believed.

The pageantry and gaiety of the occasion appealed to Jim. He was involved in anything that had a flare or show to it. He loved sports and was an expert swordsman and horseman. His performance was graceful and daring.

While he did many things for show, he kept his high sense of humor about himself as well as about others. He was steadfast and loyal to his friends. He attended the frivolous teas and parties given by the pretty girls of Columbia. He was a handsome, dashing figure wherever he went.

One of Jim's college activities was as a member of the Clariosophic Literary Society. There were two oratory societies, Clariosophic and Euphradian. Each student had to belong to one or the other. The two clubs served as combinations of political, social, fraternal, and intellectual clubs.

The experiences of open debate among the intellectuals was valuable to Jim. He loved the challenge of debate, the battle of witty minds. He developed an eloquence of speech which aided him as a lawyer. He was able to express himself dramatically and convincingly.

Rules of oral presentations were not always followed by Jim and his friends. Orators and debators were scheduled to speak for only fifteen minutes. Jim often became so involved that he spoke thirty to forty-five minutes. Only the shrill tone of the dinner bell stopped him.

At the time of Jim's student days at South Carolina College, Dr. Thomas Cooper was president of the college. Cooper was a professor of chemistry and political economy besides lecturing on geology. Cooper was believed to have originated the plan of nullification.

By the plan of nullification, if a state did not agree with a Federal law, it would not accept it, "nullifying" or disregarding it in the state.

Many people in South Carolina had been opposed to the Federal government from the time South Carolina became a state in 1788. When tariffs, duties or taxes on imported and exported goods became higher and higher, the state's business suffered. Opposition to the Federal government grew stronger.

Cooper's plan of nullification was supported by John C. Calhoun. Calhoun was Secretary of War until he won the vice-presidency under John Quincy Adams in 1824. In 1828, he teamed with Andrew Jackson and won the vice-presidency again. Calhoun was a South Carolinian and was angry about the tariff laws. He felt the northern states had passed unfair laws which harmed the cotton industry in the south, particularly South Carolina.

Congress passed a tariff law labeled the "tariff of abominations." Calhoun prepared a document known as the "South Carolina Exposition." The fight that had been a scuffle turned into war. Some people were talking of secession. Calhoun suggested South Carolina nullify the tariff law rather than secede from the Union. President Jackson was furious with Calhoun. He warned that the law would be enforced. He also took steps to make sure the tariff would be collected at the port of Charleston. Congress passed a Force Bill to support Jackson's position. It became clear that resistance was unwise.

Jim Bonham supported Cooper and Calhoun in their position of nullification movement. But James Butler Bonham, the rebel, could not be involved in only one rebellion at a time. He had to multiply his problems.

He organized the "Black Shirts" at the college. The Black Shirts were a group of malcontents — dissatisfied students — who rebelled against school authority. They all wore black shirts as a symbol of their revolt.

They demanded more rights. They wanted to have a part in deciding college rules and practices. They demanded better food. They wanted variety and excellence in their food at the college's dining hall. They demanded more freedom. They wanted to do away with some of the college's requirements and restrictions upon their private lives.

The school administration demanded that the Black Shirts leave school. Three freshmen, six sophomores, fourteen juniors and twenty-three seniors were expelled. Among the seniors was James Butler Bonham.

Just as the toad in Jim's field school days did not excite all of the anger in Jim's teacher, being a Black Shirt did not call for expulsion. It was a combination of things.

The Black Shirts were too open in their protests to ignore, and the group was too outspoken in its political beliefs. They practiced the doctrines of nullification and secession taught by President Cooper. Their open rebellion against the authority of the college and the authority of the state caused their expulsion.

Several students who were expelled were to become well known in South Carolina. Jim's roommate was James P. Carroll, who later became a distinguished jurist; a writer of law. William H. Gist was to become governor of South Carolina and a distinguished jurist. Francis W. Pickens followed William H. Gist as governor.

Jim Bonham lived in one of the greatest periods of

lawmaking in the legal history of America. When the first colonists came to America, they adopted English Common Law. They had no other reference of law by which they could govern themselves.

After the American Revolution, new communities developed rapidly. Many times the communities were isolated from governing bodies. There was no independent body of American law.

The English rules did not always fit the needs of the adventurous Americans. The Common Law did not have rules for homesteading. The law did not provide for the buying and selling of property which included slaves. The inheritance laws needed to be revised to include the wife and children of a second marriage. Many women died in childbirth and most of the men married quickly to provide a mother for their orphaned children and a helpmate. By the English rules only the children by the first marriage had a legal right to inherit their father's property. The new frontier created situations that were not covered or were unfair by English law.

There were less than a dozen volumes of American law in print in the early 1800s. Bonham and his college friends lived in a time of a critical spirit of the law. They questioned the important rules of the English Common Law.

The 1820s also was a great period of social spirit. The Americans began feeling their power. They could elect anyone as a judge. The politicians began to recognize the power of the voting public.

The law appealed to the intellectuals of the day. When Jim Bonham and his friends were expelled from school, the study of law appealed to their rebellious spirits as well as to their active minds. There were few trained lawyers. The young men were bright enough to study law and set up their own practices. Several became jurists, and writers of the law.

Judges and lawyers, particularly in the South, were able, brilliant and liberal. They enjoyed social and political prestige, which appealed to Jim Bonham.

Jim had a fiery nature and was stirred quickly to battle. He was impulsive and dogmatic. Once he made up his mind, he steered the same course regardless of the consequences.

He thrived on rebellion. He didn't worry about the outcome because he believed in what he was doing. The rebellious nature that made his life exciting and full would be the same nature that led him to his final rebellion against the Mexicans.

CHAPTER 4

The Rebel Lawyer

At twenty-three years of age, James Butler Bonham was an extraordinarily handsome man. He was brave to rashness. He was six feet two inches tall. He was a powerful man who stood straight as an Indian. His black hair and eyes were dramatic in his rugged face.

As a promising young lawyer in Pendleton, South Carolina, Bonham was one of the most sought after bachelors in the community. He had studied law and was admitted to the bar in 1830.

From the opening of his law office in Pendleton, he had a large and varied practice but not much money. He was a friend of the oppressed and the down-and-out who he insisted were as good as anyone else and entitled to the same courtesy and respect.

Bonham's fights were not limited to individuals' battles with the law. He was still involved in South Carolina's battle of nullification.

It was not by accident that he chose to settle in Pendleton. John C. Calhoun, Vice-President of the United States, also had a law office there, and a family residence at Fort Hill, a few miles from Pendleton. Calhoun was well known for his fight for states' rights.

Robert Young Hayne, a Democratic senator from South Carolina, kept the battle going in the Senate. He opposed the tariff bills as being unfair to the South. The issue of slavery was creating more problems. Hayne argued that slavery concerned individual states and the Federal government should stay out of it.

Hayne resigned the Senate in 1832, and was elected governor of South Carolina that year. The same year he was a part of a nullification convention. The order of nullification was passed by the convention.

Before Governor Hamilton turned over his office to Hayne, he organized a militia to meet force with force. President Andrew Jackson had stationed troops at the Port of Charleston to enforce the tariff laws. The Hamilton militia was ordered to Charleston to stop the collecting of taxes.

Hamilton appointed Jim Bonham an aide to the governor with the rank of lieutenant colonel. Bonham was sent immediately to Charleston, to participate in the battle which was soon to take place.

Bonham served as captain of an artillery battery, a company of young men from Charleston. He loved the excitement of the trip and the anticipation of the battle. He was a dashing artillery officer in his uniform with a bright red sash and silver epaulets.

Bonham and his eager young company waited impatiently for a battle which never took place. A compromise tariff in 1833, postponed the struggle. The tariff was greatly reduced. There was no need for a fight. A disappointed Jim Bonham returned to Pendleton.

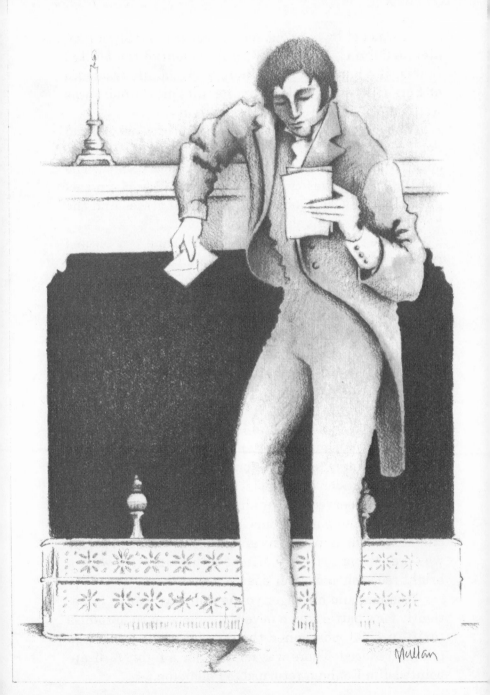

Bonham receives letter from Travis about events in Texas

For a few years he continued his large law practice. He was paid very little money because most of his clients had no money. He sometimes took goods or stock that he could trade or sell for cash. He was well-liked and did not lack for a social life and favors by admirers. He was able to dress well and present himself as successful.

During that time his rebellious nature got him into trouble with the law. One of his clients was a woman who had once been wealthy and prominent in the town but was poor by some misfortune. The opposing attorney made insulting remarks about the woman. Bonham insisted the attorney apologize or he would horsewhip him. The attorney refused to apologize. Bonham dragged out the lawyer and horsewhipped him outside the courtroom.

The judge in the case was angry. He was angry with the client because he had once tried to court her and had been rejected. He was angry with Bonham for taking the law into his own hands. He had Bonham brought before the bench.

"You, *sir,* will make a public apology immediately," the judge ordered the haughty Bonham.

"I will not apologize," Bonham refused and added, "furthermore, I am going to pull your nose."

Bonham proceeded to lean across the bench and caught the surprised judge by the nose between finger and thumb. He gave the nose a good pinch before he gave it a good pull.

The startled judge stammered and sputtered. His nose grew red and his eyes watered.

Bonham stepped back, dusted his lapels, and straightened his coat. There was a rebellious gleam in his eyes.

"You . . . you young whippersnapper! Ninety days in jail for contempt of court!" the judge yelled over the laughter of the people in the courtroom.

All of the women, young and old, were angry beyond words. They showered Bonham with all kinds of food, the best the community had to offer and far more than he could eat. They decorated his cell with fresh flower arrangements each day. They furnished him clean linens for his bed every night. His clothing was taken away and washed and perfumed.

All of the girls loved Jim Bonham *except* one. That one was the only girl he loved. He courted Caroline Taliaferro, a beautiful belle of the countryside.

Caroline was courted by many beaus. All of the eligible bachelors, young and old, in the community came to call on her.

Bonham's heart would thud as he watched her dance the Virginia Reel. He waited in anticipation all evening for one short waltz in which he could touch her tiny waist and hold her gloved hand in his. The candlelight of the ballroom danced on her rosy cheeks. Her blonde curls fell down her slender neck and moved to the rhythm of the music. She danced and flirted with all of the single men.

When banns were posted notifying the community that Caroline was marrying Dr. Miller, Bonham decided to leave Pendleton.

Jim Bonham, the handsome, sought after bachelor, was not one to leave town wearing his rejected love on his sleeve for everyone to see. Before he left he attended Caroline's wedding — escorting a beautiful girl.

With a determined look of appearing happy, he went to St. Paul's Church to watch his love marry another man. The wedding reception was at Ashtabula, a beautiful old plantation. The rolling lawn in front of the large house was filled with colorful awnings to protect the guests from the sun. Black slaves in snow-white coats and black trousers carried trays of cool drinks among the guests. Tables laden with food were scattered under the awnings.

When Bonham took the lovely bride's hand to wish her well, he knew he had made the right decision to leave. He would rather never see her again — than see her married to another.

A sadder Jim Bonham moved to Alabama in 1834. He carried on the same kind of law practice as in Pendleton. He was the champion of the underdog. And he had little money.

He wrote to his mother that he considered "the climate unhealthy." He told her that his half-brother John "was doing well, though not exactly pleased with public housekeeping." John was also an attorney.

Bonham was a man of warm affections and strong family loyalties. He kept up with each of his brothers and sisters and their families.

His brother Simeon lived in Alabama, and had kept contact with the Travis family. It was through family members that the two friends made contact again.

Buck Travis, often now called Will, wrote to Bonham about the Texas situation. The Mexicans had imprisoned Stephen F. Austin. Upon Austin's release and return to Texas, the Texans began to prepare for war. Travis recounted the glories of Texas, her struggles, her hopes for independence, and ended with "stirring times are afoot here; come to Texas and take a hand in affairs."

Bonham read and reread the letter. Each time he read it, his excitement grew. He made up his mind, and wrote to Sam Houston at San Felipe, "Permit me through you to volunteer my services in the present struggle of Texas, without conditions. I shall receive nothing, either in the form of service, pay or land or rations."

Stirring times were in Texas. It was the place for adventurous men. Great opportunities lay ahead for the strong and determined. It was the place of rebellion!

Bonham abandoned his law practice in Alabama and

returned to South Carolina. He would not leave for Texas without saying goodbye to his mother.

"I've never asked you to give up a dream, but do you have to go so far?" Sophia asked her son, who towered over her small frame.

"It isn't the end of the world, just a good strong fight for independence," Bonham smiled at his mother. "Who knows, when this thing is over, you may want to join me."

Mother and son wandered over the yards of the family plantation. Bonham turned his eyes toward the two-story frame house. He wondered if he would see another like it. No nails had been used to build the house, only wooden pegs. The chimneys of large fireplaces at each end of the structure opened to fireplaces on the upper floor. The handcarved mantle pieces over the fireplaces were unequaled in the community. The bannister of the stairway was smooth with age and wear but just as strong as when it was put in place.

His gaze moved from the house to the family cemetery. His mother did not have to tell him she would never move to Texas. He knew that her life was on the family plantation.

Bonham put aside his mother's fears for his trip, to raise money to go to Texas. When the family accepted he was going, they all helped him gather the things he would need. Milledge loaned him the necessary money.

The family gathered on the porch after bidding Bonham a fond farewell. The rising sun lighted their tearful faces as he turned to wave goodbye. He loved his family, but a rebellion had begun in Texas. He was going to be a part of it.

CHAPTER 5

The Rebel Hero

Bonham responded to the Texas rebellion as dry twigs respond to fire. His nature blazed to meet the challenge of a fight. On October 20, 1835, he organized a company of volunteers in Mobile, Alabama. News of the Mexican's defeat in a minor skirmish at Gonzales, had spread like wildfire through the United States.

The first battle of the revolution was on October 2, 1835. The Mexicans had given the settlers at Gonzales a cannon to protect them from the Indians. The Mexicans, afraid the settlers would turn the cannon on them, demanded that it be returned. The Texans refused. When the Mexicans came to take the cannon, the Texans won the battle.

All over the United States, *Help Texas* Meetings were held. Volunteer companies were formed. They headed west to "fight for freedom in Texas."

Bonham did not command the company he organized, but he traveled with them. He was pleased to travel with the Mobile Greys under Captain Burkes's command. Bonham was well-liked because of his outgoing personality.

From San Felipe, Governor Smith wrote to the Provisional Council on November 28, 1835: "Some of the Mobile volunteers have arrived in this town."

On November 30, James Walker Fannin wrote to Governor Smith: "Allow me to name to you in an especial manner my friend Major James B. Bonham, just arrived from the U. States and who enters warmly into the good cause. The Artillery is also his favorite corps. . . ."

James W. Fannin and Jim Bowie were the heroes of the Battle of Concepción on October 28. They defeated Cós in a heavy early morning fog. Cós retreated to the Alamo. Sam Houston, the new commander-in-chief of the Texas army, appointed Fannin colonel of artillery in the regular army. Fannin realized the importance of a regular army. After a short leave to visit his plantation, Fannin was busy recruiting on the lower Brazos where he first met Bonham.

Bonham's lifelong friend William Barret Travis was at San Felipe, where Travis was superintendent of the recruiting office. Although they had not seen each other in years, the bond of friendship had been too strong for time to break. The two men were much alike. They both had high principles and hot tempers. They were brave to rashness.

Buck Travis was startled when the heavy wooden door of his office opened with a bang. A tall man with hands on his hips was outlined by the bright sunshine behind him.

"Is this the place for fighting men to join in the battle for freedom?" a southern voice growled at Travis.

Travis relaxed in his chair. A gleam came into his

eyes. "Yep, and that's the reason we Texans have no place for you soft southern gentlemen." He paused and said, "However, someone just mentioned we need a cook . . ."

Bonham threw his hat at Travis and hit the mark before he could finish the sentence. Both men were laughing as they first shook hands and then gave each other a bear hug.

Buck Travis had written to Jim about the Texas Revolution. He knew that the rebellion would appeal to Jim Bonham. He was not surprised when his friend appeared in Texas.

When Bonham was commissioned a lieutenant of volunteers on December 20, 1835, the Texans were still talking about Ben Milam's storming of Bexar and the Alamo. Cós had retreated to the Alamo leaving soldiers to guard the town when Bowie and Fannin defeated him at Concepción. The Texans under the command of General Edward Burleson had held their position at Concepción through the month of November. The army had grown restless and many of the regular soldiers had returned home.

Burleson ordered the remaining men to load the artillery for the trip to Gonzales. Ben Milam disagreed with him. He argued with Burleson. The Texans should storm the Alamo. Burleson refused.

Milam faced the wild frontiersmen and shouted, "Who will go with Old Ben Milam?"

Without any planned strategy about two hundred volunteers attacked the Mexican forces. The battle was the frontiersman's kind of fighting. Each worked as an individual stalking game. They ran and jumped from house to house ambushing and attacking the Mexicans. It was man-to-man combat — fighting to kill.

The Mexicans were baffled. They had never fought that way before. After six days of fighting an unseen enemy, Cós surrendered on December 10, 1835. Cós retreated to Mexico with the promise that he would never take up arms against the Texans again.

The Texans were settled at the Alamo when Bonham was commissioned with the regular army. He celebrated the capture of the Alamo and the retreat of Cós's army on December 26, 1835, at Brazoria, where he opened a law office.

Bonham sensed the fear and urgency in the military men. Jim Bowie did not believe the war was over. He felt that Bexar and Gonzales — Texas's two strongholds — should be kept firm. Houston wanted all of the forces to gather at Gonzales.

Dr. James Grant made matters worse when he took over two hundred volunteers from Bexar and looted the town of supplies and money. Grant decided to take the war to Mexico, and he led his command toward Matamoros.

The army at Bexar, now desperate for men and supplies, was left under the command of Colonel James Clinton Neill. On January 6, 1836, Neill wrote to the Council at San Felipe asking for aid. He had only 104 men who were ragged and hungry. He believed things could get no worse.

Unfortunately, things did get worse. The men expected to be paid on January 14. No money came. Twenty or so more men left for home. There were rumors that the Mexican army was moving toward Bexar. Neill commanded his remaining men to go into the Alamo. He could no longer hold both the town and the rambling old mission slightly east of the town.

Bonham was among the men that Houston gathered at Gonzales in January. Bonham had made a quick trip to the Alamo on December 30. He realized that the mission had not been built by a military people for a fortress.

Houston thought the outpost was too isolated. It was

located a hundred miles west of Gonzales. The Texas army did not have enough men to protect that much land. The Alamo should be destroyed.

Houston gave Jim Bowie a command of thirty volunteers. Bonham was one of the company. Houston liked Jim Bonham and told Bowie that "he [Bonham] ought to be made a major by all means."

Bonham and Bowie had mutual respect for each other. Bonham was pleased to become Bowie's right-hand man. He had heard of Bowie and the famous Bowie knife long before he came to Texas. On the trip from Gonzales to Bexar, Bowie kept him entertained with adventures of his life.

On January 19, 1836, Bonham arrived at the Alamo under Bowie's command. Bowie gave Sam Houston's letter to Colonel Neill. Houston's orders were very clear: Destroy the fort and pull back to Gonzales.

While Neill read the letter, Bowie and Bonham inspected the fort. The old mission, built in 1750, spread over three acres. The "plaza," a rough rectangle of bare ground, was about the size of a city block. It was surrounded by walls and buildings. On the south side was a long one-story building called the "low barracks." Adobe huts spread along the west side which was protected by a twelve-foot-high stone wall. A similar wall ran across the north side. A two-story building called the "long barracks" covered only a part of the east side. The gap left was partially protected by the Alamo church.

The two men observing the fort could not hide their dismay. The place was so big. There were no beeves for food, no firewood to combat the cold. The water supply was a ditch from the San Antonio River. It could be blocked at any time. There were not enough men to hold a fort that size. Even if they had men and artillery, there was no ammunition.

Jim Bonham looked at Bowie. He slowly and quietly repeated the resolution of Colonel Neill's men: "We consider it highly essential that the existing army remain at Bexar."

"The men have no food, no clothes, no money. To make any kind of stand would take a miracle. We'd have to have more than just supplies . . . new men, new leaders, new spirit — " Bowie seemed to be arguing with himself. Then the adventurous spirit that had saved him before lit his eyes. "But," he smiled at Bonham, "those things do happen."

Bonham watched Bowie's strategy. Bowie began doing things that had nothing to do with retreat but a lot to do with defense. Bonham found that Bowie was respected among the citizens of Bexar. After he heard about Bowie's wife and children dying in a cholera epidemic in Mexico, he understood better the changing moods and haunted looks of the big man. The local people still spoke of Ursula Veramendi, his beautiful Mexican wife.

Bowie's contact with the people aided the men at the Alamo. He found horses for long-range scouting. His Mexican friends kept him informed with news of the Mexican army. On January 22, he heard from the Navarro family that Santa Anna was marching toward Bexar with 4,600 men.

Instead of this news depressing the men at the Alamo, it spurred them to work harder. Bowie's enthusiasm was contagious. As his spirits soared, so did those of the volunteers.

While the men at the Alamo worked together, there was a battle going on outside of Bexar. There was a political battle between Governor Smith and the Provisional Council. The Council fired Smith who in turn dismissed the Council. Neither recognized the powers of the other.

On January 26, James Bonham was elected to preside over the soldiers at a rally to support Smith. The rally turned into a rousing determination to hold the Alamo. The men asked for five hundred dollars, men, guns, and ammunition. The request stated that even if money for defense did not come, "We cannot be driven from the post of honor." Bonham was the first to sign the request. Jim Bowie signed second.

Neither money nor help came to their aid. On February 2, Bowie wrote a personal letter to Governor Smith. He tried to convince Smith that Bexar was a necessary stronghold for the Texans. He concluded, "Colonel Neill and myself have come to the solemn resolution that we will rather die in these ditches than give it up to the enemy."

On February 3, William Barret Travis, with thirty men under his command, arrived at the Alamo. Bonham was pleased to see his old friend.

"Buck, we always planned to get together and set up business. I guess this is as good a place as any," Bonham laughed as he shook Travis's hand in welcome.

Travis looked around at the work going on to strengthen the fort. "Well, this isn't quite the plantation we planned, but it's for sure we're in business."

Both men knew at that moment that this could be the last business they shared. They turned from each other to face the men who had staked their lives on the success of holding the Alamo.

Now Bowie, Travis, and Bonham directed their energies to strengthening the fort. There was no turning back. They would not give up the Alamo. Retreat was not understood by rebels.

CHAPTER 6

The Rebel's Last Stand

The compound of the Alamo became a bustle of activity. Jim Bonham fit in well with the men. His good nature and excitement about the battle to come made him popular.

He worked closely with Almeron Dickinson, a young blacksmith from Gonzales. Dickinson was in charge of the artillery. He prepared eighteen cannon for battle. The cannon ranged from four-pounders to one huge gun that hurled an eighteen-pound ball.

Ammunition was very low. Sam Blair had all of the horseshoes brought to him. He chopped up the horseshoes to provide deadly grapeshot. Bonham helped divide the metal and place it with the cannon.

The cannon were all mounted in strategic points. Bonham was one of the few men present who had the artillery knowledge for the strategy planned. He placed the cannon at such places and different levels that each could be fired to strike targets on the outside of the walls surrounding the fort.

Green Jameson was a mechanically minded lawyer. He set to work to secure the fort from attack. The open gap between the church and the "low barracks" was closed by a high fence made with pointed stakes. The fence was backed by an earthen mound from which riflemen could fire at the approaching enemy. Weak spots in the wall were reinforced with sloped banks of earth held in place by timber. The men could fire in all directions from inside the walls.

Bonham was pleased with the rapid improvements of the fort. Even as he heard daily reports of Santa Anna's march, he believed they would be ready when the Mexican army arrived.

No one believed that Santa Anna would arrive in Bexar before spring. The weather was too bad. It was the worst winter that people could remember. Santa Anna had to cross a desolate part of the country. There was no grass for his animals to eat. Yet, word continued to come that Santa Anna was making rapid progress.

The work at the fort was temporarily delayed with the arrival of Davy Crockett and seventeen to twenty volunteers on February 11, 1836. Bonham had already heard about Davy Crockett, but he was happy to see Crockett in person. He knew who the frontiersman was before the dramatic man said, "Crockett's my name. My friends call me Davy. And it looks like we might become mighty close friends here."

Everyone had heard of Davy Crockett. He was already a hero in the wild frontier country. Crockett was a large man. He was handsome as well as tall. He drew attention wherever he went. He did not wear ordinary clothes.

Bonham smiled at Crockett's coonskin cap. The unusual thing about the coonskin cap was that the coon's tail was still attached, and hung longer than Crockett's long darkish-brown hair.

He wore buckskin breeches and a buckskin coat with buttons whittled from buffalo horns. He wore moccasins and leather leggings. He had a short cape of fur around his shoulders. He carried his long rifle "Betsy."

The weather was bitter cold but that didn't dampen Crockett's spirits. He kept up the spirits of the men with his tall tales of bear hunts and Indian fights.

When he told a story, his red, leathery face with high cheekbones broke into a ready grin. That always made everyone else want to laugh, too. Sometimes he pretended absolute seriousness while he told some outlandish tale. When the men listening to his story began to laugh, Crockett's own face grew more serious. He stared at the men with startled blue-gray eyes while he continued talking. That made the outrageous tale sound even funnier.

Bonham and Travis listened to Crockett's tall tales. Bonham said to Travis, "Crockett will be a good man to have when the real trouble comes. He's not one to back away from a good fight."

They knew that trouble was coming. It was just a matter of how much and when. But thoughts of Santa Anna were put aside to honor Crockett with a *fandango*.

The large party was held on the evening of February 12. It was a welcomed relief after the hard work on the fort. Bexar was noted for its beautiful women. The men danced and flirted with the town beauties. They told tall tales, each trying to outdo the other. The party had reached a peak of dancing, talk and laughter when a messenger arrived at one o'clock.

The messenger was covered with mud. His horse was lathered. He insisted on seeing Colonel Erasmo Seguin.

Seguin was not present. Travis was senior officer in Bexar. The messenger gave the letter to him.

Placido Benavides had written: "At this moment I have received a very certain notice that the commander-in-chief, Antonio Lopéz de Santa Anna, marches for the city of San Antonio to take possession thereof with 13,000 men."

Travis read the letter and passed it on to Bowie, Crockett, and Bonham. They discussed the marching troops. They figured it would take the troops at least fourteen to fifteen days to reach Bexar. There was no immediate danger. The party continued until seven o'clock the next morning.

Colonel Neill had not been consulted when the messenger arrived. The next day Neill told the men that he was leaving for home. The reason was family illness. He appointed Travis commander of the Alamo men.

Bonham saw that a crisis was coming. He sympathized with his friend William Barret Travis, but he could understand the volunteers' unhappiness. Travis had been there only a week. He was too young. Bowie was older and more experienced. He was the one who had put the fort on its feet.

Bonham was relieved when Neill put the problem before the men to vote. Bowie was elected to command the volunteers. Travis was chosen to command the regular army.

Travis and Bowie both agreed that the Alamo was the most important stronghold of Texas. It was far more important to get reinforcements than to argue over the small group they had. On February 14, they came to an agreement. They would have separate commands. Bowie commanded the volunteers. Travis commanded the regulars and the cavalry. They agreed to confer on all major actions. They wrote to Governor Smith of the agreement and informed him that "all general orders, and correspondence, will hence forth be signed by both."

Bonham served both men. He watched as Travis soon won the respect of all of the men. Travis worked constantly at his post. His concern for the welfare of the men won him new loyalties. His requests for reinforcements strengthened their conviction to hold Bexar.

Travis and Bowie did not believe that Santa Anna could reach Bexar before mid- or late March. They did not want to take chances. On February 16, they sent their best horseman, Jim Bonham, to Goliad with a message to Fannin to bring his 420 men immediately.

When Bonham left Bexar, he passed many loaded carts leaving the town. Most of the garrison of the Alamo believed the reports of the rapidly advancing Mexicans to be "Mexican lies." However, the Mexican citizens of Bexar believed the news. Those who had the means of taking their possessions and leaving were doing so. They had been present at the battle with Cós and did not want to be around for another, and bloodier, battle.

The mass exodus did not impress the men at the Alamo. Bonham had a premonition that the citizens were right. He spurred his faithful dun horse into a gallop toward Goliad.

The trip to the Presidio La Bahía, renamed Fort Defiance, took Bonham two days. He arrived on February 18, in the midst of a cold rain.

Bonham, a persuasive speaker, lost no time in trying to convince Fannin to bring his men to the aid of the Alamo.

Fannin had made a serious mistake. Instead of training his men for battle, he had been repairing the fort. He hesitated about going to Bexar. The commander, who had been an excellent captain at Concepción, could not decide on an action. Bonham knew Fannin would not lead his troops to Bexar.

Bonham did not rush back to Bexar. No matter how he told Travis, the answer to his request was the same — Fannin was not coming. A day or two would not change anything.

On February 23, he was not far from Bexar when he met Dr. John Sutherland and John Smith. The two messengers were on their way to Gonzales and Goliad with the news that Santa Anna had arrived in Bexar.

While Bonham was explaining that Fannin was not coming, the men heard a cannon boom in the distance.

"Come with us!" Sutherland told Bonham.

"You can't get through," Smith warned him. "It'll be certain death!"

Jim Bonham sat tall on his horse and looked toward the Alamo. A mischievous smile crossed his tired face as he remembered his childhood with Will Travis. "Buck and I have stuck together too long for me to turn back now. Besides, boys, this looks like it's going to be a good fight."

The messengers rode hard and fast toward their destinations. Bonham spurred his horse toward the Alamo.

The cannon fire that the men had heard was Travis's reply to Santa Anna's demand that the Texans surrender.

Bonham saw the blood-red flag flying over San Fernando Cathedral as he made a dash for the safety of the fort. The red flag meant "no quarter;" there would be no mercy for the fighting men. The firing of the cannon was Travis's way of saying, "You will have to come and get us!"

Jim Bowie had been ill when Bonham left to go to Fannin. Upon returning Bonham found Bowie too ill to command the volunteers. Early in the morning of February 24, Bowie turned over his command to Travis.

The morning was quiet but by early afternoon firing

began. The Texans occasionally answered the fire but mostly conserved their limited ammunition. It grew dark that day before they could check their losses.

Bonham reported to Travis, "None of our men have been hurt. Looks like Santa Anna has quit firing for the day."

Travis used the quiet time to write his message *To The People of Texas & All Americans in the World*. The message in part said:

> *I am besieged by a thousand or more Mexicans under Santa Anna . . . I shall never surrender or retreat. Then, I call on you in the name of liberty of patriotism & everything dear to the American character, to come to our aid with all dispatch . . . If this call is neglected, I am determined to sustain myself as long as possible & die a soldier who never forgets what is due to his own honor & that of his country —*
>
> Victory or Death
William Barret Travis
Lt. Col. Comdt.

"Victory or Death," the words which had been burned on the caps of the Swamp Fox's Brigade became Travis's battle cry. William Travis and James Bonham had idolized South Carolina's Robin Hood as youngsters. Then they had pretended to be fighters for a good cause. They were no longer pretending. The battle they were fighting was now real.

The morale of the men was kept high by Crockett's entertaining enthusiasm. They had some injuries but no deaths. Some defenders were able to slip to surrounding houses and burn them. The enemy had nothing close to the Alamo to protect them from being open targets.

The Alamo was gradually surrounded by the enemy. The cold, miserable days began to wear on the defenders. They repaired walls, dug trenches, and stacked firewood in the freezing north wind. The Mexican army increased

Bonham returns to the Alamo

in numbers each day. It seemed as if they were playing a waiting game with the Texans.

On February 27, Travis wrote another appeal for help. He chose his most trusted friend, Jim Bonham, to carry the message to Fannin at Goliad.

"If anyone can get through the Mexican lines, Jim, you can," Travis said.

Once again, Bonham mounted his spirited horse, Dun. "If God is willing, I will return."

"Tie a white handkerchief around your hat when you start back. I'll have men watching from the walls," Travis told him. "We'll see you and be ready with the gates."

The trip took Bonham four days — round trip. He raced his strong horse to Fort Defiance. He pleaded with Fannin to move without delay.

Fannin had made a feeble attempt to go to Bexar on February 26. Three of his four old and overloaded wagons had broken down. Their oxen had wandered off and they had no means of carrying supplies. They would have had to make the long trip on dried jerky that few men carried and carry as much ammunition as possible. Fannin's officers had voted to return to Fort Defiance.

All of Bonham's pleading could not convince Fannin to try the trip again. Fannin felt the Alamo should be held. But he also felt he should remain in Goliad and keep the fort to guard the coast and keep the port at Copano Bay open.

Fannin tried to persuade Bonham not to go back to certain death. "We need you here," he said, "and when we win, you can serve Texas a long time."

Bonham's reply was not recorded, but one can imagine the reply burned Fannin's ears.

Bonham had now to return to tell the men in the Alamo that no help was coming. They were doomed to die. As he rode mile after mile through the country of hostile Indians and unfriendly Mexicans, his thoughts were on the men in the Alamo.

He cursed Fannin for refusing to come. He cursed Houston for being out of touch with the Texas army. He cursed the Mexicans for demanding the Texans remain under their control. He cursed the Texans for their lack of organization and preparation for war.

As the heat of his anger gradually died to a slow burn, Bonham's thoughts returned to the men at the Alamo. He did not feel angry at those foolish, stubborn men. He felt pity for the doomed fighters and their families.

On the morning of March 3, a lone rider sat still on his horse. The large cream-colored horse and its rider looked like a statue silhouetted against the rising sun. The only movements which gave life to the man and horse were the quivering muscles of the horse and the gentle flapping of the ends of a white handkerchief tied around the felt hat of the man.

Jim Bonham had stopped his race toward Bexar on a hill that offered a distant view of the town. He heard gunshots and saw wisps of smoke disappear in the wind. It was the tenth day of the siege.

Movement in the distance caught Bonham's attention. He watched as two riders spurred their horses toward him and recognized two men from the Alamo. Samuel A. Maverick and John W. Smith joined the lone figure on the hill.

"It is suicidal to attempt to get inside the fort," Maverick said.

"Come with us. The Alamo and its men are doomed," Smith tried to reason with Bonham.

"I will report the results of my mission to Travis, or die in the attempt!" Bonham replied to their pleas. He spurred his faithful dun into a gallop.

Around eleven o'clock the sentries at the Alamo saw a lone rider leaning low on his horse and racing through the Mexican bullets. A white handkerchief tied around his hat was blowing in the cold wind.

Bonham whipped his sweat-lathered horse through the open gates and waved his hat to the sentries on the wall. When he dismounted, he realized his leg was splattered with blood. Faithful Dun stumbled and fell. His eyes rolled in fright as he quivered and gulped air. Bonham then realized that his horse had been hit by the bullets of the Mexicans. Dun had made his last trip.

Bonham had no time to grieve over his lost horse. Travis looked into the tired face of his friend and knew that help was not coming. Travis had to break the bad news to the men.

The morale of the men was fair. Thirty-two volunteers had arrived from Gonzales during Bonham's trip to Goliad. Davy Crockett occasionally grabbed an old fiddle and played a lively tune. He kept them laughing with tall tales when they were not exchanging fire with the enemy.

About mid-afternoon on March 5, there was a lull in firing. Travis called for files on parade in the courtyard. It was the most difficult moment that he had ever faced. He had to tell the men that no reinforcements were coming to their aid.

"There is no longer hope of help. Our choice is to surrender, to try to escape, or to stay and fight to the end. I am determined to stay. The choice is yours."

The legend has spread that Travis drew a line in the dirt and said, "Any man who wants to stay and fight step across this line." All men, except two, stepped across the line.

Bowie was too weak to move from his cot. He motioned to be carried. Four men picked up the cot and placed it on the opposite side of the line. Louis Rose chose to leave. He did not want to die.

The night was overcast and dark. The garrison was quiet, too quiet to keep the Texans awake.

Santa Anna had planned his final attack carefully. For twelve days and nights he had harassed the Texans. Either by guns firing or music playing, he had kept the defenders from sleeping. When the tired Texans finally slept, the Mexican army surrounded the Alamo with more forces.

At the first light of dawn on March 6, the Texans were awakened abruptly by the harsh bugle call of the Mexican army. The bugle blast was picked up and echoed by camps on each side of the fort. The pounding of thousands of Mexican feet charging the fort joined the echo of the bugles.

The most bloodcurdling sound of all was the Mexican band playing the *Deguello*. The "fire and death" battle theme of Santa Anna, like the red flag, meant no quarter — no mercy.

The Texans beat back the first attack by the deadly aim of the frontiersmen and the cannon on top of the chapel. The frontiersmen picked off the men trying to scale the wall one by one. Bonham, Almeron Dickinson, and Gregorio Esparza, could fire over the walls in three directions.

The Mexicans retreated but quickly attacked again. The Texans fought off the attack in the same way as before. The Mexicans once more retreated. Santa Anna knew that he had to change strategy. His men were beginning to realize that it was suicidal to try to scale the walls. Hundreds of the soldiers lay dead between them and the fort.

A third attack was planned. The Mexicans were to storm the fort from all four sides. Before the Texans could shift positions, the east and west sides were to move to join the northern column. The southern attack was to move quickly to the west to capture the Texans' most important cannon. The men were to step over their dead comrades and push on. There was no turning back.

The Mexicans took their punishment as the three columns joined to rush the fort. The Texans could not move their artillery in time to stop the swarming enemy troops. The riflemen could not shoot and reload often enough to keep the enemy from scaling the walls.

Bonham saw his friend Buck Travis fall from the north wall with a bullet hole in his head. He knew the defenders could not stop the angry Mexicans.

He joined Dickinson on a platform in the back of the church. Just below, Gregorio Esparza worked his small gun by the south window. Robert Evans kept the ammunition coming from the powder magazine by the entrance.

Nails and scrap iron flew from the cannon. The enemy in the plaza were hit, many killed. Colonel Morales, protected by his soldiers' fire, moved the Texans' eighteen-pounder to face the church. He opened fire, raking the church — the timber platform, the thick stone walls, the strong oak doors.

Bonham fell. His last rebellious stand ended.

By 6:30 A.M. on the bright, beautiful morning of March 6, 1836, all was quiet at the Alamo. The Texans had been defeated. All were dead. Santa Anna ordered all bodies to be stacked in a funeral pyre and burned. Among the Mexican soldiers stacking bodies one wore a felt hat tied with a white handkerchief.

James Butler Bonham was consistent in his actions for his short twenty-nine years. He rebelled against formal school as a child. He rebelled against the administrative authority in college. He was ready to rebel against

the federal government during the nullification contro-
versy. He rebelled against the ruling of a judge in the
courtroom. He rebelled against Mexican authority in
Texas.

His name is embedded in the history of Texas. He rebelled against the oblivion of death — and won. James
Butler Bonham will never be forgotten.

BIBLIOGRAPHY

Adair, A. Garland and Crockett, Sr., M. H., Editors. *Heroes of the Alamo*. New York: Exposition Press, 1957. E. C. Barker Texas History Center. The University of Texas, Austin.

Barker, Eugene C., Editor. "A Critical Study of the Siege of the Alamo," *The Southwestern Historical Quarterly, Vol. XXXV, July, 1931, to April, 1932*. Austin: The Texas State Historical Association, 1932. E. C. Barker Texas History Center. The University of Texas, Austin.

Bonham, James Butler, Alamo Heroes (Biography) Clipping File. Library of the Daughters of Republic of Texas at the Alamo, San Antonio, Texas.

————, James Butler, Vertical File. E. C. Barker Texas History Center. The University of Texas, Austin.

Butterfield, Jack C. "Beau Gest in Texas" (unpublished manuscript). Library of the Daughters of Republic of Texas at the Alamo, San Antonio, Texas.

Carpenter, Alan. *South Carolina*. Chicago: Childrens Press, 1967.

Fehrenbach, T. R. *Lone Star: A History of Texas and The Texans*. New York: Macmillan Company, 1969.

Frantz, Joe B. and others. *Heroes of Texas*. Waco: Texian Press, 1979.

Hart, Albert Bushell, Editor. *Source-Book of American History*. New York: Macmillan Company, 1899.

Hollis, Daniel Walker. "The Cult of the Oratory," *South Carolina College Vol. I*. Columbia: University of South Carolina Press, 1951. Newberry-Saluda Regional Library.

Johnson, William Weber. *The Birth of Texas*. Cambridge: Riverside Press, 1960.

Lord, Walter. *A Time to Stand*. New York: Harper and Brothers, 1964.

Monaghan, Jay. *The Book of the American West*. New York: Julian Messner, Inc., 1963.

Nevin, David. *The Texans*. New York: Time-Life Books, 1975.

Stevenson, B.A., M.A., Anna B. *Beans From the Lone Star*. San Antonio: The Naylor Company, 1949.

Tinkle, Lon. *The Valiant Few: Crisis at The Alamo*. New York: Macmillan Company, 1964.

Webb, Walter Prescott, Editor-in-Chief. *The Handbook of Texas, Vols. I and II*. Austin, Texas: The Texas State Historical Association, 1952.